Why I

An old acquaintance recently has become a good friend. He has done me a huge favor because he asks questions that challenge me on how I know I've heard God. His name is Don Bridger.

He pins me down. His are not easy questions. Our approach to knowing God has been quite different. I had to explain my answers to him in greater depth and with greater certainty of my convictions than with people in my own church. Don and I seem to speak different languages.

At first, his questions frustrated and annoyed me. Then I realized he was not coming against me. He was sincerely interested in how I could be so certain that God was instructing me to do a thing. Especially something that, in view of my circumstances, did not seem to him to be practical or wise. They seemed to involve thoughtless risks.

Sharing some of my personal experiences with Don helped clarify how I had come to understand God's personal and specific instructions to me. Don began to realize that the path I had taken had somehow given me confidence so that I recognized when it was God and when it was not.

I came to understand through him and others how much we all want a reality relationship with God, who speaks to our inner person. He's there for us.

I have written these stories prayerfully in hopes they will encourage you to take chances on hearing God as He speaks to you also. It will involve risk. But it's worth it.

Grider Thrasher

Live BEYOND the water's edge —

Endorsements:

I was inspired when I read... this book and learned how God has been leading (Grider) on one 'risky' journey after another, and has used him to proclaim God's love as Jesus revealed it. I think you will find, as I have, that this book is not only interesting and inspiring, it challenges us to live boldly, trusting in God's presence and power.

– Dr. Boyce Bowdon, retired United
Methodist minister, Oklahoma City, Okla.

'Risky Faith' will whet your appetite for living in the Spirit by faith. All of Grider's stories are true adventures of living by faith, living by the leading of the Holy Spirit's guidance. Grider's visits to us in Russia endeared him to many and proved that he is a man willing to risk for Jesus. These adventures are waiting for every Christian who wants to step out of a dull, boring, empty life into a life filled with excitement.

– Edgar Norris, Missionary in Russia, WIM, RMAI
Sr. Pastor of Slovo Xhristovo and WCCI,
Kursk, Russia

A reality relationship with God is valid and strong and amazing in Manchester, Tenn., or Morocco or Spain or Russia or wherever. In a highly interesting and convincing way, Grider Thrasher shares that truth with the reader....

– Worth W. Gibson, retired pastor,
Jonesboro, Ark.

Risky Faith

COVER PICTURE

Author Grider Thrasher, age 70, hangs upside down from the limbs of a dogwood tree in his yard to illustrate risk. Natural faith assured him he could safely lock his feet around the limbs as he did as a child. Norman Dickson, photographer, took the picture in May, 2007.

Dismounting, Grider landed on his shoulder and face, rather than hands and feet as he intended. Nevertheless, he was safe, receiving only a dirt smudge on his shirt and no bodily harm. Faith from a scriptural perspective is based on the knowledge of God, his promises and directives. From a natural perspective, acting on it seems risky.

A Reality Relationship With God

GRIDER THRASHER

Book design and graphics by Bill Young
Photography by Norman Dickson

ISBN 978-1-4276-2301-0
For Worldwide Distribution
Printed in the U. S. A.

Library of Congress Cataloguing in Publication Data

Thrasher, Grider
Risky Faith: a reality relationship with God.
A personal journey in hearing God and acting upon it.

ISBN
1. Faith - spiritual verus natural - Christianity   2. Spiritual
life - Christianity.   3. God - Will.   I. Title.

Dedication to a very special Lady

It was September, 1955, when I first saw pretty, petite, dark-haired Sally. Two years later she was my wife. But for several months after that encounter, it looked extremely unlikely.

The setting was Missouri Methodist Church, Columbia, Mo., where Wesley Foundation for the three campuses of Stephens College, Christian College and University of Missouri, was housed. I was introduced to Sally at a supper in the fellowship hall, but I had no confidence to talk to her in front of her friends.

I confessed to two male friends that I was interested in her and they were quick to declare that I couldn't get to first base. Being more than a little competitive, I bet them I could walk her back to her Stephens' dorm that very night. I couldn't believe I said that, but once the gauntlet was thrown down, I did not hedge on the challenge.

A hamburger, fries and milk shake were on the line when I saw her about to leave. I yelled down the hall, "Sally! Wait!"

She stopped. "What did you say?" she asked.

"Could I walk you back to your dorm?" I choked out the invitation, expecting rejection but favored with agreement instead.

Back at Stephens, we definitely did not hit it off as we tried to get acquainted. It seemed impossible that a relationship could develop between us. Nevertheless, next day I called her and asked her out. With a polite excuse, she declined. We continued to talk a few minutes with a bit more civility than the night before.

The following day, I called her again to ask for a date. Different excuse, same result.

My fragile ego never had let me give a girl a chance to turn me down more than twice. This time I did, calling her 14 days to no avail. Even so, we talked a while each time. We did not argue, but it was not exactly warm and fuzzy either. She still did not agree to a date.

After the first four attempts, I was convinced that she never would say, "Yes." I decided to annoy her by making her turn me down 20 times. But I didn't get the chance. Her mother became ill and Sally left school before my 15th attempt. She returned home to Liberal, Kans. Sadly, her mother died and Sally stayed home with her dad. I did not see her again that year.

Upon reflection, I certainly was not mature enough that Fall to develop a meaningful relationship with her. Had we dated, probably nothing would have come of it. Instead, as the second semester began, I saw her through the crowd, across the big room at Wesley Foundation, and was all a-flutter, heart pounding.

I went over to her, expressed sincere compassion for her loss and, right in front of the guy she was talking to, asked her out for a Coke. She accepted. We were both different that night and became inseparable. Months later, I asked her to marry me.

Life and marriage have not always been easy for us, but she stuck with me when it was not comfortable and when our words to each other seemed only to produce confusion and agitation. It seemed hopeless for a period of our lives, but God kept us together when we were confused, frustrated, angry, and eager to escape each other. Nonetheless, "I do" and "I will" were covenant words for us, even though we did not know then what "covenant" was about.

Sally is my partner for life. She has been glue and inspiration, encouragement and determination as wife, mother, grandmother and friend. Next to the Lord Jesus Christ, I owe her everything – not by obligation, but by my realization of, personal desire for, and response to her own incredible love.

Thank you, Sally, desire of my youth, delight of my latter years. I love you.

Grider

Acknowledgments

This book would not have been possible without the help of many people. Some are mentioned below. They have been tremendous help and inspiration.

Dr. Mike Murdock, The Wisdom Center, Ft. Worth, Texas encouraged me during his School of Ministry that I had a book in me that others would want to read. He showed me how to write and publish my own book.

Joe and Brenda Pace of Joint Heirs Ministry made the first contribution to help with publishing costs. They've supplied years of encouragement.

Linette Brown, stepped out in faith, believing God to provide her money to help sponsor publication. God came through and she came through.

Bill Young spent countless hours designing and redesigning graphics and PDF files. Norman Dickson photographed me for the cover, helped with cover graphics and became a sponsor.

Dr. Jim Stillwell, professor at Arkansas State University, used his red marking pen to make considerable grammar and rewrite recommendations. Alan Patteson, Jr., pushed me to a higher level of storytelling effectiveness. Angel Lovelace was a source of constant encouragement as she poured me coffee at Joe Muggs and read bits and pieces as I'd make changes. She is also a sponsor.

Dale and Janice Walker, Pastor John Turner, Todd Alexander, Ron White, Lynn Ratliff, and Hubert Brodell are also sponsors, who have endured my constant conversation about the book, along with readers Thurman Burman, Jesse George, Kelly Freier, Stephen Northcutt, Marjorie Taylor, Ron Young, Jennifer Simmons, Kim Liddell, Lori Sexton, Al Padek, Amelia Rainwater, Tyra Murray, Mike Doyle, and Rick White.

Don Bridger prodded, read a manuscript, and encouraged me. His daughter, Dana Hurt, designed cover art that I ultimately elected to save for another book.

Pastor Steve Farmer, Pastor Worth Gibson, Pastor Boyce Bowdon, and missionary pastors to Russia, Edgar and Pamela Norris, have reviewed copies of the manuscript in various stages and kindly offered comments for publication.

F. Clift Richards, CEO, Victory House Publishers in Tulsa, former president of Harrison House, gave me considerable insight on avenues for publication and marketing.

I hope I've not left anyone out. Thanks so much to all of you for incredible assistance. I could not have done this without you.

Grider

Table of Contents

Common sense argues with its weapons of reason and logic that you should not proceed by faith.

But that is anti-God

1

Beyond the Water's Edge

"When I saw Jesus far out on the water shrouded in mist, I wanted desperately to get to Him. But my companions merely thought I was seeing a ghostly apparition. They were afraid.

"I tried not to let them see it in me, but I was also afraid.

"Of what? The unknown 'person' off in the distance? Or of not getting to Jesus when He was that near? If it was Him.

"Everybody knows I'm impetuous. I was at this moment, too.

"I jumped to my feet, leaned over the starboard side of our small ship past the drying fishnets, peered across the sea and cried out, 'Jesus! Jesus! Jesus! Is that you? If it is, bid me come!'

"It was him. He called out to me to come join him.

"I couldn't get over the side fast enough. I did not exit the ship into the water, but onto it. That's right! Onto the water. I walked quickly towards Jesus. Wow! Imagine that! Me! Simon Peter. Walking on water."

You know the rest of the story. Jesus was still there for him when Simon Peter eventually turned his eyes back to his circumstances and incurred the results of seeing with his natural eyes and natural mind. Fear set him up for a sinking sensation.

Never have I been more eager but also more fearful than when deciding whether I heard God instructing me to do something, which I then proceeded to do. Taking action that threatened real danger. You have to do that by faith.

Faith is a journey that is full of potentially perilous risks as the natural mind sees things. Common sense argues with its weapons of reason and logic that you should not proceed by faith. The argument is that faith was okay for stories in the Bible, but that we are not living in Bible days any more. As a result, we are urged to employ intelligence and knowledge and disregard anything else.

But that approach is anti-God. Paul's letter to the church at Galatia re-certifies the words of Jesus that *"the just shall live by faith."* *(Galatians 3:14 KJV)* The "just" are those who have accepted Jesus as Savior and Lord. The "just" bow their knees and proclaim their sovereignty to His Lordship. Most people who read this book are probably the "just."

The command to all of us is to live by faith. To do so requires that we be willing to release our tight hold on what is readily known to the natural mind and reach beyond the limitations of mere intelligence to grasp the unseen and unknown. It means to trust the Holy Spirit's prompting even though the natural human way seems more appropriate at the moment and His way often does not make natural sense.

Marching seven days around the walled city of Jericho and, finally, blowing the trumpets and shouting at the top of their lungs, made no natural sense to the biblical children of Israel. But their obedience to God's direction produced victory without a fight.

Priests stepping down into the torrential flood waters of the Jordan River with the ark of the covenant on their shoulders did not make natural sense. The priests and the ark would surely be swept away, drowned and destroyed. But their obedience to God not only stilled the flood, but rolled the waters back so that more than two million people could cross safely into Canaan land which God had promised them.

Faith is never seen. What is seen, is not faith. You can't have faith in or for something you already see and have. Faith is unseen. That can be scary. Faith begins where the will of God is known. His will is disclosed in scripture, but some things pertaining to specifics for our individual lives are made known by the Holy Spirit to the hidden man of our heart. They are never in conflict with the Bible. God reveals Himself as One who produces through people that which is unbelievable and seems impossible. Our actions that flow out of our faith make it possible.

This book is a picture of my and my wife, Sally's journey into the risky realm of faith, though it is too short to be all-inclusive. It also tells how we were led to believe we heard God and how He birthed in us the courage to act on what we believed we heard.

Though faith is risky, trying to live without it is far more hazardous. My prayer is that these stories will encourage you to come to know in a greater way the real joys of living by faith.

Questions
for Personal Reflection

⊗ How do you feel about my statement that God is still speaking to individuals today?

⊗ Have you ever experienced "knowing" God was directing you to do something?

2

The Dead Mouse Lives!

Probably nobody was as surprised as Pat Boone when the actor took his daughter's stricken mouse in his hands and prayed. The mouse had been dead for at least 30 minutes when he was met with the tiny lifeless rodent and his child's grief.

As I heard the famous actor recount the story, I ordinarily would have listened in total disbelief, even been inclined to mock him, were it not for his sincerity and my being an invited guest. Instead, at this noon luncheon occasion in Washington, D.C., I found myself listening with riveted intrigue, knowing in my heart it was true when he revealed the mouse fully recovered. Imagine that! A mouse raised from the dead!

Pat Boone's experience with the mouse stretched his growing faith; hearing about it stretched mine. I had to decide on the spot whether to believe God would do such a thing today. I could only listen with my heart, because I was not familiar with scriptures that might help my decision.

How much impact that had on my life is partly revealed in the personal stories in this book. I did believe what he said. I would never be the same. What was birthed in me that day was a strong desire to search for more stories of present day miracles – not the kind people speak of regarding discovery of a wonderful new drug with all its harmful side effects – not the stories of new heart and cancer procedures that temporarily postpone deadly problems.

I'm grateful for the breakthroughs in medicine, electronics, and other technology. But I'm talking about incidents beyond the reach and scope of all those things. Stories where only God could be the answer, as all else failed. The obvious source was stories in the Bible, which I now believe to be absolutely true. But that still left unanswered the question, "Will He still do those things today?" My unqualified answer is that He will in your life and mine if we will dare to expect Him to do so.

In the last chapter of Mark, Jesus said, *"These signs shall follow them that believe,"* *(Mark 16:17 KJV)*. We believe sometimes without giving much thought. Belief is just in us. It's there. Other times we must deliberately choose to believe. I am convinced we have to deliberately choose to believe that we are among "them" in this context. That is what enables us to step out in faith with a strong confidence that the rest of His statement shall be true in our lives.

Have all my prayers resulted in absolute, instant changing of the situation for which I prayed? Many of them have, but not all. Is it because God is either uninterested or unwilling? No. Are there things we still do not know? Yes.

Sometimes I have to re-read and proclaim scriptural promises and refuse to say or believe anything else until I see God's hand at work. That's not 'conjuring up faith.' It is my way of encouraging myself in the Lord. The example is King David for whom all seemed hopeless and lost when his army returned from victory in battle to discover their village of Ziklag was burned and their families were kidnapped. (See 1 Samuel 30:6) He encouraged himself in the Lord.

No matter what the results seem to be, I'd rather continue to pray and expect that God will be there in every situation than to shrug my shoulders and absorb a licking because I didn't ask. I've never prayed for a dead mouse, but that's not to say I won't.

Questions
for personal reflection:

✠ Consider Pat Boone's story about the dead mouse – Did you find yourself refusing to believe it? Or did you think it might be possible? Do you think I was naive to accept his word for it? Deep down, honestly, would you like to have that kind of faith?

✠ Do you reject or do you believe, as I do, that Jesus might have included us in the following statement? *"These signs shall follow them that believe,"* (Mark 16:17 KJV).

"The only fraud was what the devil was trying to put into my mind."

3

Oral Roberts Said What?

Young evangelist Oral Roberts seemed to be a fraud in the days I had watched him on black and white television. But God has convinced me that the only fraud was what the devil was trying to put in my head.

Isn't it funny how God sometimes will use a person you did not appreciate to come to your aid in a vital moment? Oral Roberts came to my aid.

He is not a fraud. He has been hounded by critics, but has done what he "knew" God directed him to do, accomplishing far more than those who criticized him.

When I was employed by The United States Jaycees, I was far off target in completing a "Leadership in Action" book for the organization. Our Executive Vice President finally came down hard on me and imposed a strict new deadline whose ultimatum meant 'put up or shut up'– perform by his deadline or be fired. I had two weeks and I knew I couldn't possibly finish that soon, even working almost around the clock, weekends and all.

Matters were complicated by the well-meaning intrusion of friends. It was Sunday night and they dropped in unexpectedly to visit. I was slumped in a chair exhausted.

Before they left, Peggy Wilbanks put a paperback in my hands that she said I absolutely had to read now. I had no idea at the time that my friends were hearing God when they came unexpectedly.

She didn't mean to, but she was pressuring me big time. Friendship with her and her husband, David, seemed almost at stake if I didn't read it. It seemed grossly unfair at the time. I had known them 17 years, since my freshman year in college, but if I refused to read the book, I believed it might strain the relationship. Still, I knew I had neither the time nor energy to read any book.

Nevertheless, I attempted to scan Oral Roberts' book, "The Miracle of Seed Faith" while my wife, Sally, took her bedtime bath. When I opened the book, it appeared that Peggy must have underlined some phrases and I could glance at what was underlined and absorb enough to talk about it as if I had read the book. That would be deceitful on my part, but I was desperate.

Three chapters into the book, I realized Peggy hadn't underlined anything. It was printed that way, underlined by Oral Roberts, the author. Thankfully, it was so compelling that I stayed up most of the night and read purposefully until I finished the entire book. My need hooked me.

What got my attention most was his stories of people whose problems dealt with insufficient time to complete a vital task. He offered them a solution. God is the answer to all your problems. He is your source, whether you need money, favor, health or time. God established the laws of seed-time and harvest. Farmers live by it, but most church-goers are aghast at the thought of expecting God to meet their seed with his harvest.

My question now was how did it apply to me?

Here's what I learned: When we need a harvest, we need to plant a seed of like kind. Corn produces corn, strawberries produce strawberries, etc. Plant the seed, look to God as the source of our supply, then EXPECT A MIRACLE. In other words, for my immediate need, I could give away precious time to someone in need of my help and do it joyfully as unto the Lord. That's my seed.

As it is for the farmer, my harvest is ordered the moment my seed is put into the ground to die. The moment I release it from my hand and put it into God's hand, my harvest is on its way.

All seed is created with the motive and ability to produce an appropriate harvest, whether it is natural or spiritual seed. Like the farmer, if we dig up the seed, it cannot produce. Doubt is the enemy of our seed. Faith is the sunshine and rain that enables it to produce.

But how could God multiply time? Well, he did it for Joshua. *(Joshua 10:13)* Why not for me?

Next day I had opportunity to sow my time seed twice in the first hour at work. Mary ran our lunch room in the headquarters building across from Boulder Park in Tulsa, Okla. We often had conversation and on Monday morning when I arrived, I noticed that she seemed really despondent. I asked her what was bothering her. She shared it with me and I listened, offering to pray for her as I left. I was well aware of the half hour it cost me and under my breath mentioned it to the Lord as a time seed worthy of His harvest for me.

Soon after that, I was settled into my office, door locked, coffee pot perking, first of six pipes filled with tobacco from the big humidor on my desk and a haze of smoke beginning to accumulate around me.   Reading through a stack of notes from my research as I prepared to write, I was unwillingly interrupted by a pounding on the door.   It was Jim McCauley, a fellow staff officer.

My instructions to Lawanna, my secretary, had been to hold all my calls and let no one into my office.   But you couldn't expect her to stop Jim.   If the door hadn't been locked, he'd have been in before she could open her mouth or make a move.   I really felt the urgency to begin writing without delay, but the Holy Spirit reminded me about sowing seed and expecting God's miracle harvest.

The next 45 minutes were spent brainstorming with Jim to develop a membership recruitment project for local chapters.   It's ironic because he was in great standing with the Executive Vice President, who by now seemed eager to get rid of me and had made it known for some time.   All he lacked was a substantial reason.   Because of my tardiness in completing the book, it appeared that I was doomed.   I wouldn't have bet against it.

I was neither flippant nor indifferent about the prospect of losing my job.   I wanted to finish the book and keep the job.   Until now I was desperate.   But the words of Oral Roberts' book were exploding within me.   I was at a particular moment in time when I could choose between acting on that man's godly wisdom or acting under the weight of the fear and pressure that was freezing my creativity.   The choice was fairly obvious.   Do something different than what I had been doing or fail.

I chose to give my time at this moment to Jim as if it were a faith gift unto the Lord.   And I chose to expect a miracle.   It had to be a miracle because I could see no way out otherwise. So, I took a deep breath and asked Jim, "What's on your mind?" His response made his project seem so petty for the moment compared to mine. My natural mind said he ought to be helping me instead of seeking help from me.

Fearfully, I had made the right choice. I gave away more time and forced myself to be joyful about it and expect the miracle that surely could not happen. That was not confident faith. But it was all I could come up with and I acted upon it.

Three days before my "do-it-or-else" deadline I had my miracle! The book writing was finished and it was in the hands of the printer. I had time to relax before my trip and to prepare for nine days of New England seminars on leadership.

The response to the book from the national officers and the troops in the local chapters was overwhelmingly positive. I was not then and am not now that good. But God. He's amazing!

The Executive Vice President would have to do his sulking behind closed doors as I began a whole new schedule of apparently effective leadership seminars. God had given me my miracle and had heaped added blessings on top of it.

> *Here's a confession. I believe now that the Exec V-P was interested more in my success than in getting rid of me. His threat and his deadline got the best out of me for the organization's benefit. It wouldn't have been possible without "The Miracle of Seed Faith."*

Seed Faith is a three point covenant
(my explanation):

1. God is your source.

2. Sow seed according to your need; give for a specific purpose.

3. Expect a harvest. Let your words agree with your expectation and don't focus on the problem.

Questions
for Personal Reflection:

❯ What do you think about seed faith?

❯ Have you ever made a decision to trust God to meet your need in that way?

❯ Relate a personal experience with God

"Without faith, it is impossible to please God,
Because anyone who comes to Him
Must believe that He exists
and that He rewards
Those who earnestly seek Him."

(Hebrews 11:6 NSRV)

4

"See Rock City"

Advertising signs on old barn roofs finally got me in trouble. Only the older generation will remember the persistent signs along the highway between Nashville, Tenn., and Chattanooga. "See Rock City" they implored, cajoled and persuaded.

My family and I were motoring along in our old faded green Chevrolet station wagon enroute to Miami Beach. Interstate highways didn't extend to that area at the time and the signs and roof paintings were entertainment. A beach-front hotel was our destination for six nights' free lodging with only one requirement – that I tour River Ranch Acres near Orlando one day. Disney World would be nearby someday, but was still just on the drawing board.

I persuaded the family that "Rock City" would be lots of fun. It was. But I kept adding just one more cavern and mountaintop overlook until we had spent most of our first day out and were exhausted a long way from our destination.

Finally, late that night, we stopped at a motel somewhere in Georgia. We were ripe for the unexpected problem we encountered.

The glass in our faded old station wagon's dual-use rear door wouldn't roll up so we could lock up for the night. It would not be a big deal if it had happened at home. Get it fixed next day. But this was different. What to do here and now?

We intended to leave most of our luggage in the vehicle overnight, but we could take it into the room. No big deal. Except you feel vulnerable when you leave your vehicle in a motel parking lot at night with the window down. It ought to at least be your choice, but this time it was not.

When the rear window worked properly, the glass would disappear into the door, which then could either swing open or fold down. It normally worked when someone pressed a switch on the dashboard or turned a key in the door. The glass would slide into the door like any other window.

On this occasion, it went into the door, but wouldn't come back up. I tried the door key and I tried the inside switch – to no avail. I tried both again and again. Still nothing worked. Man! I was clueless, a little bit angry, and truly frustrated.

Problems always seem to know when to occur in order to create the most havoc, don't they? The glass was stuck in the door. That's when big drops of rain began to fall. Though the drops were large, they were scattered – one hitting me every now and then, constant but not yet soaking. Still, the threat of a downpour was obvious.

What should I do? I didn't want to leave the window open with it raining and I didn't know how to get it to work.

I heard myself exclaiming, "Oh, Lord, what do I do

now? Help."

How much of that was asking and how much was verbal futility, I can't honestly say. Then I heard me shout, "Sally! You and the boys come quickly!"

Her natural response was, "But it's raining!"

"That's why I need you to hurry to the car," I urgently replied. I had an idea, hopefully from God. If not, we were still in trouble.

I insisted and she and the boys somewhat grudgingly came. "Why'd you bring us out in the rain?" she asked. The boys muttered their own sleepy disapproval.

"'Cause this window is stuck and I can't lock up," I replied. "We're all gonna lay hands on the back of the car and pray and look to God to cause the glass to slide up like it usually does," I stated as if I definitely believed it would happen.

"Put your hands on the door, please." Then, I asked God in Jesus' name to cause it to work. I didn't have a formula, just a plan that if we'd touch the car and agree, He'd do it for us like Jesus said in Matthew, chapter 18. I dared to tell it to obey. What nerve!

Then I put the key in the lock, turned it and ..... whirrrrr. The glass was emerging as if nothing had ever been wrong. And we dashed for the room just before the sky poured out its rain with intensity.

True story. And it had an immediate sequel. Coincidence cannot claim responsibility for the glass only working once after we prayed. The remainder of our trip, the glass never went back up until we prayed, but it never failed to do so when we did.

There's more. After we returned home, I neglected to follow up and get the problem fixed. We went on another short trip months later to Hot Springs, Arkansas. When we picked up a passenger, we pushed the button to lower the glass and put her luggage inside. It wouldn't come back up. Since we were going to a conference called "Faith at Work," it was actually funny that we were challenged to pray over it again and apply our faith even before we arrived at the conference.

You know the obvious answer. It worked. Every time we used the window, we had to turn to prayer to get it to work. It always did. God is faithful!

It was a building block for us. The Bible declares that *"the just shall live by faith"* (Galatians 3:11 KJV) and we were learning to do so a little at a time.

It's important that we not keep our faith hidden. Let our family and others see that we believe God. As we do, our faith becomes more sure for us. We gain confidence in that realm by doing. It's risky for our reputation, but it's worth it.

Questions for Personal Reflection:

- Have you prayed a "Prayer of Agreement" as mentioned by Jesus in Matthew 18:19?

- Do you believe God is interested in our everyday situations and circumstances?

5

How Are We Going to Make It?

My stubbornness often got us in trouble.

Like running on fumes the last 20 miles with absolutely no place to get gas.

Or taking a short cut, missing the mark and being hopelessly stranded somewhere.

Or driving through soft sand at river's edge with no possibility of stopping and turning around, plunging through the water at a low point, virtually jumping the car onto the sand and gravel on the other side, and sinking the car up to the axle as darkness began to settle over us.

Somehow, with much difficulty, we came through all those scenarios. Each seemed a terrible and senseless experience at the time, but perhaps they helped breed in me a willingness to step out beyond the safe zones where I became helpless and had to trust God to get me through.

We had $20 and not even a gasoline credit card when Sally and I started to Manchester, Tenn., about a 250-mile trip. Her anxious question was, "How are we going to make it?"

I tried to hide my nervousness, "God will provide." I

hoped I wasn't lying.   But I honestly was not certain. In other times, I might even have crossed my fingers in foolish hope.

After two or three years of fretting about my business career as a commission salesman and literally stealing hours from myself each day to study the scriptures and pray, I left the company on Christmas Eve, determined to travel in ministry full time. I had, at that time, no formal training nor other preparation except those hours devouring scripture and reading faith books.   My earnings had diminished greatly and our funds were drained due to my broken focus. Not a good time to launch anything.

Did God really direct me to break away from the business world and do this full time? I didn't have a single ministry appointment lined up.   Where would I go? How would we get by financially?

Our friends, the McCaslins, had not specifically invited us to Manchester, but said we could minister in their home. They made no promises except that we could spend the night with them. Several couples from the Methodist Church would meet for regular Bible study. I was jumping at any opportunity.

But, was God really directing me to make this trip? My thoughts were wavering greatly. It was mid-January and the Lord had not appeared to me in a dream. I had not heard an audible voice. I did not have an unmistakable nudging inside me. In my thoughts, a battle was going on between hope and those practical financial issues concern-ing the wisdom of such a journey.

We might not receive a love offering.   I didn't dare

tell Sally how dire our circumstances might be. Somehow, I kept my mouth shut rather than speak doubt and unbelief at the same time I was trying to walk by faith. That would make me a double-minded man whom James wrote would receive nothing from the Lord. Plus, I really was afraid Sally would object to our going and prove to be right. I had to go forward boldly.

Driving through Nashville, we could have been killed. Instead, it was not us, but our doubt, that died in an improbable instant.

We were beside an 18-wheeler as we started into a sharp curve under a railroad track. That's when we were suddenly blinded by an intense water spray. We couldn't see the truck on the inside of the curve, only its swirling fog and sheets of water on my windshield. We appeared destined to be crushed by even the slightest brush with the 18-wheeler or we might slam into a piling as the water hydroplaned us under the railroad track somewhere immediately ahead.

Suddenly, Sally shouted, "I see an angel on our hood! He's huge and he's just sitting there with his arms folded as if to say, 'I've got things under control, folks.'"

All doubt about our safety and God's call and provision vanished. Whether we actually had heard God or not, He was with us and would make a way. What a wonderful God we serve.

Financial provision? We didn't ask for anything, but people gave us well over $300. God no doubt met us in Manchester and began to unveil a road map for our immediate future.

By faith, we opened ourselves up to be directed by the Holy Spirit. Nothing's better.

**Questions
for Personal Reflection:**

✗○ Have you ever been aware of the possibility an angel might be nearby to help you in a situation? Did you visually experience that presence?

✗○ Have you set out to do something where you knew you would fail if God didn't come through?

6

Surprise In Sioux Falls

It's not easy for a "nobody" to get preaching engagements, but God seems to delight in turning our "dead ends" into amazing opportunities. That happened for us in Sioux Falls, S.D.

I had tried to move into full time traveling ministry without the benefit of a confirmed schedule. No dates were penciled into my calendar. I did not have a group of people ready to support my efforts with prayer or money. Sally traveled with me at that time, but we were on our own, floundering, unaware of the foolishness of it. All wisdom appeared to have deserted me. But I had to do this, I thought.

A Jonesboro friend, Mac Jaramillo, made some phone calls and persuaded his brother-in-law and a pastor friend to open some ministry doors for us in Colorado. We can't say what the people received except that we were not invited back. Financially, we hardly made traveling expenses and received nothing for ongoing bills back home. Despite that, it was more devastating to our confidence than to our pocketbook.

We went from Colorado to Sioux Falls, S.D., without a ministry engagement, just a limited promise from friends that we could stay with them a few days. There was not even as much promise as there had been previously at Manchester, Tenn. It was not what we were hoping for, but we didn't know what else to do at that time. Our choice was to go there or go back home feeling defeated and thinking we had totally missed God.

This was not Sally's vision. She was trying to be supportive of mine, but Sally had trouble understanding why I insisted on going to Sioux Falls, despite considerable uneasiness. It was a long trip and we'd still have a long journey home.

When we arrived, we learned that the Hodges had not felt comfortable to ask their pastor if we could preach there. They didn't mention us to him at all.

My disappointment was almost crushing, but it was good to see the Hodges. I dared not show my near discouragement. We hung out with them Friday and Saturday, tried to just relax in the Lord. Sunday morning we went to their church, our minds still full of conflicting thoughts about what we were doing there and what we should do next.

We were not prepared for what happened at the conclusion of the service. Bill and Sue introduced us to their pastor as we were leaving. He asked, "What are you doing this evening?"

"Going on to Minnesota," I replied.

"When do you have to be there?" he wanted to know. That put me on the spot.

"Nothing definite," I said, not really wanting him to know we were not scheduled anywhere. He probably sensed it, though. Was I uncomfortable? Absolutely. I was cornered and torn between being honest with him and trying to hide my lack of direction.

He broke the tension for me. "Why don't you stay and preach here?" I wanted to shout.

Sally and I looked at each other. "Sure," I said, "Thanks for the invitation." *"Humble yourself in the sight of God and He will lift you up."* (James 4:10 KJV) I remembered that later.

I don't know what I preached that night. I don't even recall if we prayed for people at the altar. But I do remember that afterward the pastor asked if we were poor. I unhesitatingly declared, "No!" *"Let the poor say I am rich."* (Joel 3:10 KJV) I didn't feel rich and I didn't remember the scripture, but somehow I knew I had to respond that way.

He then admonished his congregation, "We're not giving to the poor tonight, but to an anointed man of God. He's good soil and has sowed a good word among us. Your gift to him will not merely be returned, but multiplied." Wow! Satan's attacks against my thoughts vanished instantly! God hadn't taken a vacation! He was indeed *"directing our path"* (Proverbs 3:6 KJV) and *"ordering our steps."* (Psalm 37:23 KJV)

Jesus put it something like this (my words and interpretation), "Sometimes you have to ask. Not doing so is often the reason you don't receive. Other times you must be more forceful and seek. Then you will find what you seek. In this case, we had to knock and the door was opened to us." The name of this church was "Open Door Church." Ironic, isn't it?

We received more than $400. That was a large,

generous offering for that time. God rewarded our hearts and encouraged us greatly. He also let us know that things are not always as they appear and that, though some do not enthusiastically receive us, others do. Faith always involves action on our part. And it is risky business. *"Without faith, it is impossible to please God."* (Hebrews 11:6 KJV)

All those things were a blessing. But I just realized in writing this chapter that the focus of God on our going to Sioux Falls was to hear a pastor declare me to be an anointed man of God. It's the *"anointing that breaks the yoke"* of bondage and sets at liberty those that are bound. *(Isaiah 10:27 KJV)*

THE LESSON I LEARNED:

We don't have to know the end result from the beginning in order to follow God. And people don't have to know us until God hooks us up with them by His Spirit. We were in Sioux Falls by the fact that He ordered our steps. Inexperience created many doubts within us about the wisdom of our decision to go there on a promise of nothing.

But God had a pastor waiting for us, sensitive to the Spirit's leading, to ask us to preach. It wasn't just for our benefit. It was mutual. It was a God thing.

God knew the end before the beginning. We persisted despite a battle with uncertainty. As we follow God, that will be true as often as not. It requires us to put our confidence in Him. And it inspires us as we discover an ability to rely on Him.

Questions
for Personal Reflection:

➤ Has God ever turned a "dead end" into an amazing opportunity for you?

➤ Have you found that you usually flow best with the Holy Spirit after you set out to go somewhere?

STANDING OVER THEM WERE SOLDIERS ARMED WITH AK-47S

7

Jesus in a Muslim School

Fear fired a shot across our bow more than once after we arrived in the Islamic North African nation of Morocco. Thank God, the story did not end there.

Though fear tried again and again, it failed. The Holy Spirit did more than we expected. He is declared to be *"able to accomplish abundantly far more than all we can ask or imagine." (Ephesians 3:20 NRSV)*

For me, everything up to now had been just a series of small confidence builders compared to what was about to happen in the ancient walled city of Marrakesh in the summer of 1997.

Seven people were on a prayer trek for a week in the major cities of Morocco, dressed and acting as tourists through Tangier, Fez, Rabat, Casablanca and Marrakesh. The entire mission was one of praying for the people and leaders and students in that nation. We prayed inside and around key landmarks, government structures, mosques and universities. We were engaging in spiritual warfare through prayer. We did *"not wage war after human standards; for the weapons of our warfare are not merely human, but they have divine power to destroy strong holds."*   *(2 Corinthians 10:3,4 NRSV)*

We were a non-existent group prior to meeting each other in Malaga, Spain, at an appointed time. A girl in her early 20s from western Washington, a man in his 30s from Virginia, a mid-40s Mexican man living legally in California, an Egyptian in his early 40s, a Kansas City woman who had been a missionary in Athens, Greece for 14 years, an American man in his early 30s who was a co-missionary in Greece. And, of course, me. I was a 60-year-old from Jonesboro, Ark. Our only connection was that we all had met one or both of the missionaries.

We didn't meet each other until we arrived in Spain, most of us at the Malaga airport, though the Egyptian, Moushir, was unheard from and finally met us 36 hours later. Even the missionaries were not at the airport in Malaga to meet us as planned, because they missed their flight and caught up later. It was the kind of beginning where everything seemed to go wrong. I don't think the "*principalities.....powers.....rulers of darkness.....spiritual wickedness in high places*" *(Ephesians 6:12 KJV)* were thrilled about our intrusion into their realm.

We took a bus along that Mediterranean strip known as the Costa del Sol (sun coast) to Algeciras, a port city near the Rock of Gibraltar and opposite Tangier, Morocco. When Moushir finally arrived, we boarded a late-night ferry to cross the Mediterranean. All our missed connections and confusion to that point were nothing compared to what was coming.

Fear fired its first shot across our bow to turn us away from our mission as we departed the ferry about Midnight. Walking about 500 feet along an elevated pier to the customs building, we looked below and saw people with luggage open and belongings scattered. They may have been smugglers; we didn't know, but standing over them were soldiers armed with AK-47s.

Our inner turbulence finally began to subside as one by one we were passed through customs with our luggage open on a conveyor.   Then another shot of fear was fired as the man from Virginia was pulled aside, questioned and searched thoroughly. Moushir stepped up to interpret and discovered that a black bag containing his movie camera had aroused suspicion. He was cleared and we set out to find transportation, pre-arranged but nowhere to be seen, then or ever.

The Bibles I had hidden in my bags apparently went unnoticed. We had been advised by the missionaries, Brian and Gail, that we could be imprisoned if they were discovered or if we tried to give them to the 'wrong' people. Their admonition was that we be sure we were led by the Holy Spirit before distributing any. After I returned home, a new friend from England I met on the trip, Graeme, was caught with a boat load of Bibles and imprisoned for about a year even though English and American diplomats pressed for his release. But our small supply raised no red flags.

Mercedes taxis took us to a hotel where our 'reserved' rooms were unheard of. More than an hour later, about 2:30 a.m., after much argument from Moushir, we had a place to sleep in Tangier, very nice rooms at that.

With walled cities from the 7th century, Morocco is a beautiful country that includes the Atlantic Ocean on the West and the Mediterranean Sea across the North. It also includes rolling hills, desert and plains. The country is an Arabian monarchy in North Africa, run by the king, heavily influenced and largely controlled by Islam, but friendly to the United States. What that has meant for centuries is that Christians are welcome if they are tourists and do not attempt to share the gospel nor give tracts or Bibles to the people.

Five days into our trip south from Tangier, we passed through Marrakesh's massive walls....walls at least 50-feet thick but including niches for vendors....to a school of the Qu'ran that was recessed for the summer. The school was available for tours. Since Gail and Brian had been there several times before, we gathered instead in a small corridor upstairs for a time of group devotional.

For safety reasons, we had always before stayed in pairs. This time we split up and I walked alone from tiny cubicle to tiny cubicle to pray as I felt led. The cubicles housed two people during school term, providing space only for a mat apiece used both for sleeping and for prayer five times a day. A tiny window overlooking a narrow alley-street provided almost no light. As I began to pray intensely, I could almost sense the presence of the vacationing students.

I placed my hands on doors and doorways and concrete bunks and moved slowly and prayerfully from one to another. After a time, I started 'pleading the blood' of Jesus over the rooms and the students that would occupy them. (According to Revelation 12:11, believers overcome the devil by the blood of the Lamb and the word of their testimony.) As I did, inspiration hit me. The following results provide their own ample evidence that it was a God thing.

As I went in and out of the cubicles and along narrow corridors, I began to sing hymns about the blood of Jesus and the power in the blood. People who know me understand that singing is not something others ask me to do.

I passed a French-speaking group and kept right on singing. If any understood English, a tiny seed was planted. But I did not inquire. I just kept going for several minutes.

I was suddenly startled by the appearance of two young men coming from a side corridor. One of them asked in English, "What's that you sing?"

I told them I was singing about the blood of Jesus who takes away the sins of the whole world.

They told me they believe Jesus was a prophet, but that Mohammed was the last great prophet. (Muslims have their greatest hang-up over Jesus' crucifixion and resurrection.) They began a friendly sharing of the Qu'ran and I responded with Bible. It was not an argument, but it was religious posturing.

Then I noticed the hands of one of the young men. They were badly burned. I asked him about it and he told me the story. When he had finished, I told him that Jesus "*went about healing all that were sick* (or injured) *and oppressed by the devil.*" *(Acts 10:38 KJV)*

I looked Abdul in the eyes and said, "I believe God will heal you if you let me pray for you. Jesus said we believers were to lay hands on the sick or injured in His name and they would recover. Do you want your hands to be made whole?"

Religion dropped its argument for a moment when this man's pressing need became the issue. "Yes," he replied.

I looked at his companion, Faud, and said, "God is going to show you by this sign who is the great God, the true God. Not to impress you with His power, but because of

His love for you both and because I have chosen to believe and act on His Word and on the name of His begotten son, Jesus Christ of Nazareth."(Islam refuses to accept Jesus as the Son of God.)

Before I prayed, I instructed Abdul briefly and requested and received permission to "pray as I pray, in the name of Jesus." He acknowledged approval. Don't worry about Islam or any other religion at this point. Let's move on to badly burned hands being made whole.

I asked him to place his very tender, very marred hands on my outstretched hands. He did, not even realizing that in that simple, obedient act he was adding his faith to mine. (Obedience to a man of God's instructions brings faith to an action level.)

James wrote in his epistle that *"the effectual fervent prayer of a righteous man avails much." (James 5:16 KJV)* I believed James. And I knew that I qualified as a righteous man because Jesus *"became sin for me that I might become the righteousness of God in Him."(2 Corinthians 5:21 KJV)* The word interpreted "avail" means an unleashing of power like when dynamite is exploded.

Truthfully, my faith was tempted to waver and nullify the whole thing before I began to pray. I told Abdul that often the results are instant but sometimes they come after a brief delay. I assured him that the healing would, nevertheless, surely come. The moment I began to pray, my faith rose up powerfully. I didn't worry about whether Abdul's hands showed it at that moment, I had God's assurance within me.

When I looked at Abdul's hands afterward and saw

little or no change, he said, "When I get home, my hands will be healed." His faith spoke agreement with my faith. It was not mere idle words; he really believed it, too.

Just before we parted, I looked at Faud and told him, "You will see his new skin and healed hands and then have to make a decision what to do about Jesus." I spoke that in humility, not pride. My confidence and my authority were in God.

They both nodded. I know it was accomplished. Not because of me, but because the Word of the Lord is true. It is *"lively, powerful, and sharper than a two-edged sword."* *(Hebrews 4:12)*

Paul said, *"I come to you not in persuasive words of man's wisdom, but in demonstration of the Spirit and of power."* *(1 Corinthians 2:4 KJV)* I could never have persuaded Faud and Abdul to receive Christ as Savior, but by daring to proclaim His healing power as evidence of His love, a seed was planted that could change a nation.

I am persuaded that if we have nothing more to offer the world than our argument about the sacrifice and resurrection, people like Abdul and Faud will remain convinced that their arguments about Allah and Mohammed are more believable. And they will die in their sin.

The power of the resurrection is the same power that works in us, according to Paul's letter to the Ephesians, chapter one. And that is the power of God for salvation. That's what I believe.

We don't always have to see the results of our praying. Our job is to follow God and do what the Holy Spirit prompts. His job is to make His word true. We are partners that way.

"We proclaim His word and He confirms it." (Mark 16:20 my paraphrase)

Questions
for Personal Reflection:

✕ Have you had an experience of sharing your faith with a Muslim? Or other unbelievers?

✕ Do you believe that Jesus is the way, the truth, and the life; and that no man comes to the Father (God) except by Him?

✕ What is your honest 'take' on my story of boldly proclaiming God's healing power for Abdul and praying for that with confidence?

8

Where You Park Matters

God has *"plans to prosper us and not to harm us. He has plans to bring us to an expected result." (Jeremiah 29:11 my paraphrase)* Jeremiah prophesied that. It was not just for the people of his day and immediately beyond. It is a revelation of who God was, is and forever shall be. The prophecy is for all of us, too.

Many things were happening under the Holy Spirit's anointing in my local church in Jonesboro, Ark., where I was an elder in the year 2000. Many gifts of the Holy Spirit were in evidence as my pastor and I and others ministered the word and trained people for prayer ministry at the altar.

But I was chomping at the bit to be fulfilling my own dream of going to the nations. Still, I had no specific direction at that point.

A September journey to Russia began to materialize out of nothing that June. It was not what I expected at that time. The restless urging of the Holy Spirit compelled me to attend a three-day ministers' conference in Tulsa, Okla. Our financial circumstances screamed loudly against my going anywhere. Questions came from family, "Why are you going? How do you know you heard God?"

I couldn't give a good answer. I just knew that I

couldn't skip the International Charismatic Bible Ministriess (ICBM) annual gathering at the Mabee Center at Oral Roberts University. I had an overwhelming desire to go. I believed God had something special for me there. And I really needed whatever it was.

Timing looked awful, but it turned out to be perfect. Obedience to seemingly unimportant little things prompted by the Holy Spirit positions us to do greater things.

I arrived well before the start of the first session and could have parked almost at the front door, but God had other plans for me. As I pulled up close, I had a sense that I should reserve those spaces for people who came later. Only when I finally settled on the space in the farthest corner of the parking lot a few steps from Lewis Avenue, did I apparently find the spot God must have intended for me.

That seemed to be confirmed soon after the first session ended. When I walked the considerable distance to my car, a high-pitched car horn caused me to nearly jump out of my skin. Annoyance turned to delight when I recognized my good friend and former Rhema Bible Training Center classmate, Ed Norris, a missionary to Russia, whom I had not expected to see there.

We were both there alone and on our way to supper before the evening session. Timing was perfect for us to eat together.

As we talked about a lot of things, a growing desire began rising up inside me to help him in Russia for a while and to do it soon. I didn't know how he might use me, but I couldn't deny the powerful intensity I was beginning to feel about it. Never having had Russia on my heart before,

I timidly approached him about it, wanting to be of help but not impose on him and his family.

Ed was noncommittal about the whole thing. Not even saying he'd like for me to come. Soon after we left the restaurant, I began to realize that he wanted no part of telling me what to do. I had to hear from God and be willing to speak it.

Over our meal, he insisted I tell him when I wanted to come. He wouldn't suggest a date nor length of stay. I hesitated, then nervously replied, "How about late September or early October?"

"How long do you want to stay?" he responded.

I gulped and said, "Is four or five weeks too long?" I didn't know where that came from, except it had to be deep inside me. It had to be God.

The Psalmist said to *"delight yourself in the Lord and He shall give you the desires of your heart."* (Psalm 37:4 KJV) This was happening so fast I wasn't certain where the desire came from, but I was about to find out the Holy Spirit was prompting me. Had I spent time considering all the ramifications, I might have reasoned myself right out of going.

Ed said, "Perfect. I'm starting a Bible training school on October 1st and you can arrive a couple of days before and teach with me the first four weeks." He added, "I do need the help, but God had to be the one directing you, not me."

As uncomfortable as I was speaking first during this exchange with Ed, I would discover soon enough it was the easy part. When I began the process of trying to get things in order for the trip, I learned how determined the devil was that I would not make it. That will be revealed in the next chapter.

Looking back, I have pondered some scriptures that are so important for us to know and rely upon as we seek to follow God. Where the devil is concerned, *"we are not ignorant of his devices."* *(2 Corinthians 2:11 KJV)* The remembrance of those words reminds us his plots are to create turmoil and confusion. Our response is to recognize it comes from him and decline to be overwhelmed by his ploy. We also must refuse to hold people accountable for their unwitting part in it.

Vital to our success is the knowledge that "greater is He that is in us than he that is in the world." *(Philippians 4:19 KJV)*

Jesus painted a picture of sheep and the good shepherd in John chapter 10. We are those sheep. The fourth verse reveals that we know His voice and follow Him. Verse five can set us at ease, *"And a stranger will they not follow, but will flee from him: for they know not the voice of strangers."* *(John 10:5 KJV)*

As we take steps to follow the unction in our inner man, we increase our confidence that we know His voice. *"We have an unction from the Holy One"* *(1 John 2:20 KJV)* The Greek word is "chrisma" from which the Charismatic Movement gets its name. An alternate to unction is *"anointing"* *(The Strongest Strong's Exhaustive Concordance of the Bible, copyright 2001 by Zondervan).*

I could not stay firm in my decision to go to Russia unless I knew I was obeying God. The actual trip begins in the next chapter.

Questions
for Personal Reflection:

✕◯ Looking back, are there times when you have experienced that unction?

✕◯ Have you ever been put on the spot to respond to someone like Ed in hopes you were really hearing God? Relate it to others.

I repented of
speaking the problems
to all who
would
listen.

9

All Things Are Possible

Things are not always as they appear. Thank God!

Y2K was not devastating to America, the world, the banking system, anything. Chaos did not prevail except in doomsday warnings. Once the actual event passed and sabotage had not had its way, people settled again into their normal lives. The world had survived

If appearances were really truth, I'd never have made it to Russia late in 2000. Anxiety stalked me for a time. Going to Russia seemed impossible. But a change in what I was believing and saying turned circumstances around.

I repented of speaking the problems to all who would listen while I tried to get a Russian entry visa. I made a decision to quit looking at what seemed impossible, *"for with God all things are possible."* (*Matthew 19:46 KJV*)

I was not unaware of Satan's devices -- his tricks to get us to agree with all the bad he'd try to get us to fall into; I knew about them. I knew most of all that if he got me to use my mouth to speak failure and defeat, that's what I'd end up having. I could not allow that attitude to rule. So, I began speaking instead that everything would be in hand when I needed it. Not to worry.

Some Russian requirements were unexpected by me. Their laws are different from ours. Their approach is different. Like it or not, I had to do it their way. And develop a good attitude about it. That was a challenge for me.

None of my other travels, for example, required an Official Letter of Invitation issued by a registered organization, as was the case in Russia. Application for an entry visa must include that Letter. I was frustrated in late August and most of September by confusion over that Letter, especially determining appropriate fees for the Letter and the visa, which could range from $50 each to over $300.

What I let really set me off was an email failure for days between Ed Norris in Russia and myself. We couldn't communicate at a time when I thought I needed someone to hold my hand. But it was time for Grider to grow up and deal with those things.

Days before my scheduled departure, it looked impossible. If the devil was ever in anything, it appeared that he was in that red tape on this occasion. I helped him attack me by telling and retelling the challenges as if they were absolutely defeating me. Accusations, even in blowing off steam to people who aren't involved, are not the vehicle to faith and favor.

I ultimately got around to encouraging myself in the Lord as David did and e-mailed Ed Norris, the missionary I would be working with, proclaiming that everything would arrive on time. Faith was speaking of *"things that were not as if they were already mine"* (Romans 4:17 my paraphrase).

I could not in my natural mind see the completion of any of those things, but faith is evidence of what is unseen. All the time my natural senses screamed that I was lying. But faith arose inside to assure me.

Though my confidence was threatened temporarily, I did not waver and finally received the visa and my tickets the afternoon before I was to fly out of Memphis. It pays to speak words of faith unwaveringly when the circumstances would produce doubt. I had learned to stay firm. A moment of wavering can undo everything.(James 1:8) I could not afford to vacillate now if I wanted to get to Russia.

When the visa and tickets arrived, I was euphoric and prayerfully primed. I sent Ed a truly inspired email. The latter part was what I would call a prophetic vision:

> "Before we met this year in Tulsa, I was praying in the spirit one morning and the Holy Spirit spoke to me that He foreknew all that I would be asked to do. And He said that He not only would speak to my heart about what to do, where to go, and when to do it; He also would speak to those whom He already had chosen to come alongside me for both prayer and financial support.

> "I began to cry as He revealed that to me. It was not on my mind that morning, but had been many times before. I knew that I could not possibly go forth into the world without a well-equipped support group. I wondered how to go about recruiting people for that purpose. But He said not to give it another

thought. He would line them up. They would come forth and let me know they had been chosen.

"They have...by the dozens. I have cried again and again, so touched by a supporting cast as I have never known before. Beyond what I could imagine. People I never would have dreamed about asking. God is so good. I don't even know all their names.

"A bunch of us really are expecting a lot from God in Kursk. Many people have already been praying for you and me for more than a month ... every day. Unasked by man. Prompted by the Holy One.

"Oh, the enemy has tried to find ways to make us anxious or discouraged these last few days. Putting sickness on both my sons and three of my grandchildren, causing our heat and air system fan to eat up bearings to the tune of about $300, causing distress in Sally's car, etc.

"But God is whom we believe and He says to disregard such things as no more than a squawking bird. He has healed the sick and provided funds for the mechanical things. We know that His word will not return to Him void, but will accomplish the thing(s) He sent it (His word) to do. He sent His word and healed us. He wishes above all things that we prosper and be in health as our souls prosper. You know: (3 John 2).

"I leave here with great confidence that He not only has gone
before, but is stationed at our hind-
quarters as well. He spoke a word to
me twice not to worry about Sally;
she would be well cared for, as all
my family would be.

The following is actual prophesy:

"Even now I see a vision: it is
rainy and a man with a kite (like
the Benjamin Franklin discovery
of electricity) that is struck by
lightning. It is in the city of
Kursk. It is power from the throne
of the Most High God. It will bring
more light and life than electricity
has. And the light will be the light
of men (Jesus) and it will overcome
the darkness.

Now I see after the initial
flash, succeeding flashes, followed
by a glow on the horizon as noticed
when it otherwise is completely dark.
That glow is growing both upward and
outward and is engulfing a city and
a nation. It is spreading quickly.
Pockets of it are extremely luminous.
Pockets of it are constantly flashing.
They are brilliant and refuse to be
smothered in the darkness. They
move around from place to place. But
they will not be put out. They will
not be dimmed. The nighttime will
become so bright that one can read
fine print without any other light.

"And I see a burning. Such a
brilliant hue. But no smoke. It is a
consuming fire, but no person on whom
it settles is burned. But neither
will such a one ever be the same
again. The prayers of the righteous
have been heard. They have ascended
to the throne. And the King of Glory
has issued a decree. And mighty ones
have been sent forth to assist the
saints in declaring and demonstrat-
ing the wholeness and completeness of
His salvation. Praise be to God!"

End of the prophesy. And the email to Ed.

I was already on fire. And more prepared for teaching,
preaching, and even healing and miracles than I realized. I
would see the evidence over the next 35 days. Many things
would rise up to try to take away the Word and the anointing
that was in me. Nevertheless, my faith was stirred and God
was strengthening me. I would not be the one to accomplish
the things He had spoken to my heart. He would do it and
get all the glory.

I did not know there was a medical university in Kursk
that attracted students from across the world because it
conducted classes in English and was affordable. Reports
since then from Kursk disclose that Kursk Medical
University students from African nations and the Pacific
rim already have gone back to their home countries with the
light of the gospel.

In addition, the Norris family has made at least two
trips to the students' countries and been allowed to minister
to their families and others. Many of them were Buddhists,
Hindus, and Muslims before encountering the Norris' and

The Word.   Many are since changed by the gospel that originated for them in Kursk.   Only God knew that would happen.

Questions
for Personal Reflection:

✝ I had to change what I was saying about the problems and start speaking in 'past perfect tense' – *"calling things that were not"* yet as though they already had come to pass. *(Romans 4:17 my paraphrase)*   In reading that, how did it make you feel (what did you think)?

✝ How did you respond to my printed prophetic utterance? Do you believe that God still works through people in that gifting today?

✝ Have you ever prophesied under the anointing/ gifting of the Holy Spirit as mentioned in the 12th chapter of 1st Corinthians? Would you like more information about it with Bible texts?

> ### *But the young man with black hair, a black outfit and a homemade "Welcome Grider" sign was not to be found*

"Grider's visits to us in Russia endeared him to many and proved that he is a man willing to risk for Jesus."

– Edgar Norris, Missionary in Russia, WIM, RMAI
Sr. Pastor of Slovo Xhristovo/WCCI, Kursk, Russia

"Grider is one who dares to live in the Risk Zone with God."

– Pamela Norris,
Pastor, Word of Christ Church Int'l, Kursk, Russia

10

Stranded at Sheremetyevo

Flying into Russia for the first time ever was a big deal. The airport on the outskirts of the city of 12-million people is known as Sheremetyevo. It is one of several commercial airports that serves Moscow.

The approach our plane took did not put me in position to get an aerial view of the inner city. Had it done so, I would have seen a colorful myriad of the twisting onion domes of St. Basil's Cathedral at one end of Red Square. Lenin's mausoleum, nearby, would be dwarfed by the Kremlin, a huge fortress housing the seat of government. The Moskva (Moscow) River would meander below the other side of the Kremlin.

The first time I walked alongside those extremely high Kremlin walls, I broke into singing, "*A Mighty Fortress Is Our God.*" I thought of verses in scripture that speak of Him being our High Tower and such. Kremlin was one of the most imposing earthly embodiments of that picture that I ever saw. I didn't realize that day that the Kremlin and St. Basil's were built a few hundred years before communism took them over.

As I departed the plane at Sheremetyevo, I saw nothing particularly unique to Russia, except printed words on the signs. I couldn't read them, so I followed the other passengers to the baggage pickup carousel, waited for my two bags with a degree of nervousness, and found a place in line, where I finally presented my passport and visa to armed security. That was the easy part.

Next, I placed my bags on a conveyor to be opened and examined before pushing through the exit gate. At the moment I passed through that gate, I was really in Russia. Re-entry through that gate was not permitted.

That's the place where a mountain of despair tried to erupt around me. Many people were waiting to greet arriving passengers, but the young man with black hair, a black outfit, and a homemade "Welcome Grider" sign was not to be found. Ed's last e-mail had described Vlad, a young co-worker who would meet me and take me on an overnight train to Kursk. He was not there.

Suddenly, I was swarmed by a group of men shouting, "Tax-i, Tax-i, Tax-i." It must have been obvious I was an American. In Russian-accented English they insisted, "Your friend is not coming. We will take you to a hotel."

But that wouldn't work. Neither Ed nor Vlad would know where I was and I did not have a clue how to get in touch with either one of them.

I couldn't pick up a telephone in Russia with much chance of getting help in English unless I knew the word, 'ponglisky', which I couldn't remember in that confusion. Besides, a card was required for the particular pay station to be used. I didn't know that then. Also, I had not acquired Russian Rubles yet. So I was more helpless than I imagined.

All those obstacles could be overcome, but not with my state of mind at the moment. As I kept brushing off over-zealous cabbies, my mind was going a thousand directions at once. I was inwardly shaken. I could not think clearly in the confusion of such cacophony.

Finally, with my feet through the straps of my luggage, I leaned against a wall where I could watch people. I took a deep breath and prayed and prayed and prayed. When my mind could not focus on how to pray, I began to pray in the language given by the Spirit who knows how to pray when we're not sure *(Romans 8:26)*.

Peace came over me like you wouldn't believe unless you found yourself in a similar situation. Suddenly my mind was clear and I began to recall scriptures that pertained to my circumstances.

I began verbally to remind myself of God's promises. Isaiah declared that *"No weapon formed against you shall prosper."* *(Isaiah 54:17 KJV)* The Psalmist said that *"though a thousand fall at your side and ten thousand at your right hand, it shall not come near you,"* *(Psalm 91:7 KJV)* and *"He whose mind is stayed on thee shall be kept in perfect peace."* *(Isaiah 26:3 KJV)*

After a half hour of this battle, the Holy Spirit prompted me to look at a young man who had just arrived. He had no welcome sign, nothing to really identify him. "Are you Vlad?" I asked. He was. His explanation? "People don't usually get through customs that fast."

God's hand was evident the entire time. We caught the overnight train to Kursk and I taught in Ed's new Bible School the next four weeks with very positive response. I preached often in a Pentecostal Church in the city and ministered in a dorm room at the medical university, where at least one Buddhist came to Jesus. Many others have followed as Ed and Pam Norris continue to minister to them.

Questions for Personal Reflection:

> Have you ever felt alone in a crowd?

> More specifically, have you been in a strange land alone in a crowd you could not understand? Where you had no clue what to do next?

> Read Philippians 4:6-8 below. What do those verses say to you about circumstances that may have overwhelmed you?

Philippians **6** *"Do not worry about anything, but in everything by prayer and supplication with thansgiving let your requests be known to God.***7** *And the peace of God, which surpasses all understanding, will guard your hearts and your minds in Christ Jesus.* **8** Finally, beloved, whatever is true, whatever is honorable, whatever is just, whatever is pure, whatever is pleasing, whatever is commendable, if there is ant excellence and if there is anything worthy of praise, think about those things.

11

Night Train to a Jewish Heart

Desperate was I to find a men's room 'indoors.' It was a very cold day in Russia near the end of my first trip to help Ed Norris in Kursk.

Snow was more than ankle deep on the grounds of the unfinished Pentecostal Church where, in an unheated room, I was teaching his Bible students. The snow had 'freshened' the smell of the outdoor toilet to the point that I could not bear going inside one more time.

Russian old men sometimes relieved themselves against a building or just out on the street. Should I do that? No chance. I was an American preacher in Russia. The consequences could be terrifying. I could not do it, though I considered hiding behind some trees or bushes. It was probably good that I found no such 'cover' on the church grounds.

I was in pain as I decided to go down the street to a nearby hospital. Hospitals do have bathroom facilities, do they not?

'Toilette' seemed to be a useful word when I used it at the reception desk. The Russian woman used several words to respond. I did not understand even one of them. She spoke no English and did not offer to show me where such facility might be. I walked up and down stairs, peered into wards, desperately looking around, but I could not identify a bathroom.

My break time was soon over and my only remaining choice was to go back into the cold, dismal room at the church building and teach for another hour. After that, Ed and I boarded the tram and bounced and jostled our way to the 'stop' a few blocks from Norris' apartment. I felt like I was about to explode when I finally reached the bathroom – thankfully not occupied.

Life in much of Russia is far different from most of these United States.

I was reminded of that failed communication experience and its pain when I prepared to board the night train to Kazan alone, with no interpreter. Nevertheless, I braved it on my third trip to Russia in 10 months. Bathrooms were in the same place on every train and were a little better than outdoor toilets.

Truthfully, I was utterly helpless, though. I did not yet know the Cyrillic alphabet of the Russian language and still could neither speak nor understand the language. How foolish was I for attempting to go a significant distance from Moscow alone?

The stroll alongside the high, intimidating walls of the Kremlin did little to assuage the underlying anxiety, though Julie was a cheerful and informative host. One day when time seemed more favorable, I would greatly desire to enter the Russian fortress in Moscow built centuries before Communism was in the mind of Karl Marx and his protégées.

Two thoughts were uppermost as the hours passed before we would head for the train station on the far east side of the huge city. I longed to see the beautiful auburn-haired Irina, whom I had met in April and her handsome husband, Ildar, whom I saw from a distance during that worship conference in St. Petersburg, but had yet to meet. They were my prime reason for going to Kazan.

Had Julie's call to their pastor's house alerted them to my soon arrival? I would regret it very much if they were not present. I sensed a strong possibility that they might not be, but I had no natural way of knowing and was committed to this trip by now.

Second on my mind on this balmy but humid day was my reluctance to leave Julie, an aide to Pastor Hugo Niekirk of South Africa. She was extremely helpful and encouraging. She also spoke both Russian and American English effectively. Who would read the signs printed in cyrillic and interpret the spoken language for me once I boarded the overnight train? I was totally helpless in Russky This was taking a step in faith that just might be too much for me.

It's probably good that I didn't know before departing Moscow on the overnight train that it was a 90% Muslim city of 3,000,000 people. Traveling with others in a Muslim country I had done, but this time I was totally alone. My inner peace was utterly threatened.

It was July 17, 2001, and I had just spent a week in Kursk with Ed Norris and his family again. Ed had left for the United States a couple days ago and I was to be in Russia for two more weeks without a preset ministry schedule and no interpreter. The next 14 days would be in territory unknown to me.

Uncertainty became my companion even as Julie had helped me get a ticket and board the Kazan train at dusk. When she unsuccessfully tried to call Irena and Ildar for me, their pastor said for me to come. Still, I had no idea what to expect, nor did I have any understanding what his expectations were.

What awaited me? Only God knew as I got on that train. More questions flooded my mind. Was I trying to push my way into a place not directed by God? Was this self-promotion?

Entering a four-person coupe, I stashed my bags under a lower bunk as the attendant took money for sheets and pillowcase and a cup of chai (tea).

I was nervous about what tomorrow would hold. Would somebody meet me at the train? If not, I had no telephone numbers nor any idea how to contact anybody. I was either traveling in total foolishness or hearing God and going in obedience. I had to trust He was the one speaking to me to do what seemed impossible. Time would prove if my decision was right.

What a relief it was when a largely obese man already in the coupe turned to me and spoke in English. He was a self-proclaimed Russian Jew, whose family was preparing to move to Germany. He confessed that he was not a religious Jew; even declared himself to be agnostic and possibly atheist. But we talked for more than an hour about Russian politics and economy.

Then came the tale of his wife's great knowledge of the

German language and her fear of speaking it. Immediately the Holy Spirit caused Paul's words to Timothy to rise up in me. I shared them with him, *"God has not given you (us) a spirit of fear (or timidity), but power and love and a sound mind."* *(2 Timothy 1:7 KJV)* I told him we could pray if it would be all right with him and God would release his wife from that fear. It's amazing how God opens doors for sharing both His great love and His great power available to believers today.

I told him distance was no obstacle for God and I said we'd pray that God would assure her that He'd given her a sound mind. God would confirm that the devil was trying to hold her back. I said that people who don't really know God are so easily frustrated by the wiles of the devil, mostly in their thoughts.

He wasn't totally believing what I was saying, but he wanted to know more. *"Let him who has ears, hear,"* *(Mark 4:9 KJV)* Jesus often said. The man was skeptical but willing. He had not encountered a man with this kind of faith before. (His words, not mine.)

I told him I'd pray, with his permission, but to be effective, I needed his consent to pray the way I pray: in the name of Jesus Christ of Nazareth. "Will that be okay?" I insisted. "Yes," he said, "but I don't believe." I replied, "That's okay. I do."

As we faced each other from our separate bunks in the coupe, he allowed me to take his hands in mine and pray. I prayed for his wife, for him, for his children. I prayed the prayer of faith that is both *"fervent and effectual"* *(James 5:16 KJV).* I prayed appropriate scriptures over them because the word of God is powerful and sharp and lively. It would leave a mark on this man's life forever. He was visibly moved, wiping tears from his eyes. He had been touched by God.

Next morning, his stop came before we could exchange full names and addresses. He and his partner were gone in a flash as he said a quick thanks and goodbye. And my journey into the unknown resumed. I felt that if nothing else happened, the whole trip was worth it for this one encounter. I believe God considers each of us so valuable to Him that He'd send someone around the world, if necessary, just to share His love with us. I also believe that timing is everything.

Questions
for Personal Reflection:

>< Are you the kind of person who's willing to journey into the unknown? How do you know? Or, why not?

>< Have you ever wished you knew how to share Christ with Jews? Or anybody? What have you done about it?

>< Are you able to pray for people 'on the spot'?

12

How Could This Be God?

I heard no explosives. I saw no guns. I felt no knife in my ribs. I saw no threatening 'gentlemen' in black suits and long black limousine. I saw no menacing group of Arabs in flowing robes, turbans, and sabres. I saw no squad of camo-clad soldiers. But my arrival in Kazan nearly blew me away.

My overnight train had just come to a stop at what apparently was my station when I thought I overheard my name 'Grider' just as a man stepped into my coupe (four-person compartment), grabbed my luggage and left the train. I didn't know what to do except try to follow rapidly. There was no communication as he walked fast for more than a block, finally stopping at the rear of a very small Russian car.

I caught up with him breathlessly as he put my gear in the back and motioned for me to get in the passenger side. I knew not what to expect. What was not – but seemed like – three hours later, we stopped on the outskirts of the city of three million people at a small house on a dirt street.

My understanding didn't improve much when we went inside, though the man's wife spoke a few words in English. She said for me to eat and sleep so that I would be ready for their all-night prayer meeting. Several minutes later, a young man came by whose English was quite good and I started to feel better about things. But he stayed only about 15 minutes, then he and the others swiftly departed without notice.

Sleep? I could not. My mind raced. What had I gotten myself into? Surely this hadn't resulted from my obeying God. I must be trying to walk on water with Jesus nowhere in sight.

Outside were more houses similar to the one in which I was deserted, but there were no people in sight, there was no place to go and nothing to do. 'Mr. Spiritual' probably would say he prayed all day, but I was restless and miserable. I did pray some, read some Word, and tried to nap, but I had no peace.

I was as marooned as if I were on a deserted island, except there were no warm ocean breezes, no roar of waves against the rocks, no majestic palm trees. Just that sandy, dirty street, the cheap little houses, and me.

The young man who spoke English knew Irena and Ildar but had no information about their whereabouts or whether they knew I was coming. I learned later that they were not in the city and did not know that I was coming until they returned from vacation soon after I left. I had a strong desire to see them. Julie told me after I returned to Moscow that they called her quite disappointed that they missed me. But we couldn't work anything out for them to come to Moscow or me to go back to Kazan.

I finally met the pastor at prayer meeting. Eventually, he asked me to preach and I was passionate about Mohammad being in the tomb and Jesus being resurrected. It was later that I learned that I was preaching in an old public theater building in a city with three million Muslims, some of whom were loitering on the street outside the theater. Did they hear? I hope so, because the *"Word of God is full of life and power, penetrating to divide spirit from soul."* (Hebrews 4:12 my paraphrase) It gives life even when we don't realize it.

Saturday afternoon Pastor Sasha (Alexander), his wife and two daughters took me to a city lake for swimming. Swallowing the water was not a good idea, but we played tag and keep away and I couldn't keep it out of my mouth. I remembered Jesus' words in the last chapter of Mark that *"if you drink any deadly poison, it shall not hurt you." (Mark 16:18 KJV)* I believed I was covered by His statement.

I preached again Sunday. That afternoon the English-speaking young man took me across the city to a building where leaders of the church's cell groups were having a training session. I spoke to them about cell-group evangelism and boldness. To close the session, I offered to lay hands on people to impart a bold evangelistic anointing upon them. I'm sure God prompted it.

One lady had something else in mind. When it was her turn, she wanted her hearing restored. Through the interpreter, she said she was totally deaf in one ear and had lost 80% of the hearing in the other ear. She got by mostly by reading lips.

I tested her by speaking with the interpreter behind her back where she couldn't read our lips. Then I laid hands on her and the power of God rose up in me as I prayed. Again behind her back, I asked her quietly if she could now hear. She said, "Ya." I told her to repeat a phrase after me that I had learned to speak in Russian. I whispered it. She repeated it perfectly. She could hear.

You can rightly guess that I'm not the healer. Jesus is. But he works through them that believe. I believe He wants to do far more through us than we give him opportunity. I pray you will be encouraged to listen intently and obey the voice of God within you. It starts with knowledge of and confidence in the written word.

Questions
for Personal Reflection:

✠ Have you had any personal experience of being in a strange country alone, isolated by a language barrier?

✠ Are you ready to rely on the words of Christ *(Mark 16:18)* about being kept from harm if you accidentally drink something harmful? Even in the midst of conflicting words of fear spoken by people? Even medical professionals?

13

Salvation Train Ride

"*If I owned that lonesome whistle,*

if that railroad train was mine... etc"

And I'd let that lonesome whistle

blow my blues away."

Gordon Jenkins, composer, 1953

Those words were part of an album called "Seven Dreams" and the tune later became the score for Johnny Cash's famous "Folsom Prison Blues" with a few word changes in the lyrics. Jenkins' wife, Beverly Mahr, sang the original.

As I rode the trains in Russia, I could almost hear Cash sing his version:

"Well, if they freed me from this prison

If that railroad train was mine... etc"

And I'd let that lonesome whistle

blow my blues away."

I've always loved railroad songs by Cash, Box-Car Willie, Willie Nelson and others. Two friends, Wade Althen and Tom Bishop, used to bring their guitars to our house and break into railroad songs like, "City of New Orleans" written in 1972 by Steve Goodman about the demise of America's railroads and made a national hit bt Arlo Guthrie. It was also a big hit for Nelson 9 years later.

"Riding on the City of New Orleans,

Illinois Central Monday morning rail...etc"

My uncle, Jim Swanner, was a railroad brakeman for 40 years on the Cottonbelt between Illmo, Mo. and Tyler, Tex. My grandparents lived in Piggott, Ark., just one block from the tracks and, when I'd visit them as a kid, I'd listen to the freights blowing their whistles as they rumbled through town, especially on hot, sultry nights in the summer.

When I was dating Sally, I'd ride the Rock Island line from Kansas City to Liberal, Kans., and back on the weekend. Railroad songs still create great memories.

I never heard those singers mention stories resembling my Russia train trips to Kursk, Kazan and Obninsk. You've already been with me on my overnight ride to Kazan, the once-great city of the Mongol Empire captured by Ivan the Great. And my overnights in and out of Kursk with Vlad and Ed.

The day train to Obninsk was totally different. When seven South Africans I met in Moscow boarded with me, it was standing-room-only. Corrie Zaayman, the group's sponsor, stood with his back to a window, his eyes in a book. His six protégées were huddled with their luggage on the floor in the front of the carriage. I stood in the aisle within shouting distance of them.

Obninsk is one of the young Russian cities established for nuclear research purposes, I was told. It is only about 60 years old. Most buildings, of course, are much newer. We would headquarter there a couple days and walk many miles across hills and meadows to tiny clusters of houses where we would go door-to-door to share the gospel. The people spoke no English and I was paired with two church people who also spoke no English. All I could do was pray.

The true purpose of my trip to Obninsk, though, became apparent on that train. Quite unsuspecting, that train ride became one man's trip to salvation. For me, it was the highlight of those three weeks in Russia.

Hanging onto a seat back as I stood in that aisle with the train cars rocking me back and forth, I was asking

God for opportunity. Suddenly I saw a light flash! When I looked toward the flash, I saw a young man as he handed a camera to one of Corrie's protégées and step back. I heard myself ask a question that made no real sense as I sprang forward, "How long have you been a licensed professional photographer?"

Who would ask a dumb question like that? It was simply what came to mind in that instant. Somehow, the young Russian partly understood and tried to respond that he was not a photographer, just a man asked to take a picture of the group. I realized that, but felt compelled to speak to him. Even a question like that would open an incredible door.

He spoke a bit of English, though insisting he didn't. I told him Jesus loved him. "Nyet," he responded, "Ya, atheist."

My answer surprised us both, "No problem. There are really only two kinds of people on this train."

"Kinds?" he interrupted.

"Types," I corrected myself. "Type One is a person who knows that Jesus loves him. Type Two is a person who is getting ready to know that Jesus loves him. Ya," I said pointing to myself, "Type One."

"Ya," he said, pointing to his chest "Type Two."

"Da," I agreed. "How would you like to become Type One?"

"Da," was his surprising response.

I shared with him what was required to become a child

of God and to really know that Jesus loved him. Then, I asked, "Is that what you want to do?"

There was no hesitation. "Da!" he replied.

I prayed for him and led him to confess Jesus as his new Lord. He immediately was filled with great joy. It happened so fast I was truly amazed. Corrie had put down his book and interpreted. Afterwards, Corrie produced a Russian Bible and they spent the next two hours reading scriptures together.

The young man left the train before we did and Corrie told me, "He is in the army stationed about 1,000 miles from here. He's on his way home to visit his mother. He has not been on this train in more than a year. In a few days, he will return to camp for another year."

Wow! What a divine appointment.

My ministry plans had come to naught. I went with Corrie to Obninsk because I had nothing else to do. God used an American and South African to point this man to Jesus. One man's life was worth God sending two other men 5,000 miles each for an appointed day so an atheist could become part of God's family through the blood of Jesus Christ.

"Indeed, God did not send the Son into the world to condemn the world, but in order that the world might be saved through him."

John 3:17 NRSV

Questions
for Personal Reflection:

⤫ Was my encounter with the Russian young man a mere coincidence? Do you think I was just trying to come up with something to justify my trip and the confidence of people who had helped me with the expenses? Or was I really led to that moment by the Holy Spirit?

⤫ Have you ever experienced an encounter like the one I described?

⤫ How much value do you think God puts on one person's life?

⤫ Are you willing to share Jesus with people no matter what the circumstances or the risk? Even though you may have to make up a lame excuse for talking with them?

14

Mighty Man of Valor

Faith was always risky for the Old Testament Hebrews. The people would not obey God consistently and it always took a man to step up by faith in their place.

One such man's attitude reminds me in some ways of me. His name is Gideon. His story begins in Judges chapter six. Israel was greatly impoverished by virtue of their enemies *"having entered into the land to destroy it."* *(Judges 6:5 KJV)* thus leaving no sustenance for Israel's livestock. Food supplies and most grains were cut off from the people. Surely, it was a desperate time.

The word of the Lord to them was that they once again had not obeyed His voice.

Along came an angel, who sat under an oak tree near where Gideon was attempting to thresh wheat by the winepress to hide it from the Midianites. Gideon was afraid the armies of Midian would commandeer his wheat. He was trying to get enough wheat to have a loaf of bread to satisfy his hunger.

But the angel appeared to him and changed all that. He told Gideon that the Lord was with him. The angel called this fearful young man a *"mighty man of valor."* *(Judges 6:12*

KJV) The angel spoke those words into Gideon's heart as a powerful seed of greatness for an assignment ordered by God.

Gideon sounded a lot like me with his response. *"If the Lord's with us, why has all this happened to us? Where are his miracles? He appears to have forsaken us."* *(My interpretation.)*

The Lord (angel) looked upon him and said, *"Go in your might and save Israel from Midian. Haven't I sent you?"* *(Judges 6:14 my paraphrase)*

Gideon (Grider also) challenged the Lord further, describing himself as being of a family poor in the half-tribe of Manasseh and that he was the least in his own family. I would say that somebody is better able, better qualified than me.

Then the Lord reassured Gideon and said, *"Surely* (you can count on this, take it to the bank) *I will be with you and you shall kill all the Midianites."* *(Judges 6:16 KJV)*

Gideon was not easily convinced. Sounds a lot like us, doesn't it? He asked for a sign that God really was saying that and really would do it. And one sign (fleece) was not enough. He had to have another one. But once convinced, he obeyed God in every detail and obtained the victory.

Gideon's orders won't be our orders and our actions won't mirror his. But they will be orders that will deliver somebody from the oppression of the devil. Success will be dependent upon our making ourselves available to God to do what He instructs.

Stories like Gideon's have inspired my faith. Pick up

your Bible and read his entire story and let God speak to your heart in the process, too.

Questions for Personal Reflection:

✗◯   Does God still use individuals today on behalf of people groups or nations as He did Gideon?

✗◯   Have you tried to hide from problems or enemies? Or camouflage the fact that you are a Christian?

✗◯   Are people, regardless of background or nationality or race, important to you? Or do you want to limit your interest and involvement to those closest to you?

> *"the Lord your God, he*
> *is the Lord in heaven above,*
> *and in earth beneath."*
>
> *Joshua 2:11 KJV*

15

Two Sets of Spies

It took two sets of spies to get the truth about the promised land adversaries.

By a vote of 10-2, the Israelites declined to go into the promised land. The testimony of those who had seen Canaan first hand was 10-2 in favor of the natural view instead of the spiritual view. Based on the testimony of those spies, the final vote was even more overwhelming. The people who heard their report voted about 2-million to three against marching on into the promised land. A fearful report led them to vote against God's direction.

That was the wrong decision and it's one that becomes a commentary on democracy. Sadly, we often vote with that same majority – even in our churches.

The story unfolds in Numbers chapter 13. Moses sent 12 men, one from each tribe, to spy out the land of Canaan in preparation for the people to go possess what God had promised. They were not ordinary men in their tribes. They were rulers. God directed Moses to appoint the chief men of each tribe. He did so and gave them specific instructions on what to see and in what order. Nothing was left to chance.

When they returned, the debriefing revealed that two of them remembered God's promise to give them the land. Their's was a faith report, relying on God's promise rather than what they saw naturally. The other 10 saw only with their natural eyes and what they saw discouraged them about their ability to take it.

The fruit and abundance in the land was incredible, but they saw the people as giants and viewed themselves as grasshoppers. We often see ourselves that way, don't we? But we need to change our glasses and get a God-view.

The result was that the people delayed receiving the promise by some 40 years. (Sadly, many preachers today discourage people from claiming the promises of God.) It didn't have to be that way then. It doesn't have to be that way now. Joshua and Caleb gave a different report and encouraged entering the land. We can do the same. We make our own choice about what to believe and what not to believe, what to say and what not to say.

Jesus had a lot to say about believing and speaking. *"Truly I tell you, if you say to this mountain (circumstance, problem), be taken up and thrown into the sea (as something that shall no longer be permitted to exist), and do not doubt in your heart, but believe that what you say will come to pass; it (what you say) will be done for you."* *(Mark 11:23 NRSV)*

Joshua and Caleb's report on the promised land is confirmed by two other spies in Joshua chapter two. Josh and Caleb had called the occupants *"bread for us: their defense is departed from them, and the Lord is with us: fear them not."* *(Numbers 14:9 KJV)*

When Joshua replaced Moses as head of Israel, he sent two spies into Canaan at the walled city of Jericho to lodge at Rahab the harlot's house. Rahab said to the men whom she hid, "*I know that the Lord has given you the land, and that your terror is fallen upon us, and that all the inhabitants of the land faint because of you. For we have heard how the Lord dried up the water of the Red sea for you* (40 years ago)." *(Joshua 2:9, 10 KJV)*

She went on to declare that "*the Lord your God, he is the Lord in heaven above, and in earth beneath.*" *(Joshua 2:11 KJV)* Based on what she had heard, she believed in God and declared it. She is found in the ancestry of Mary, mother of Jesus. She married one of those spies and came out of harlotry and into the family of God.

God long ago had declared that He would go before Israel and cause Jericho and all of Canaan to be ready to give up without a fight. But the people of Israel would not believe and give God opportunity to show them He had already fulfilled His promise.

We're no different when we choose to believe the report of the natural man instead of the report of the Lord. He has prepared the enemy to cave in and let us take our inheritance in Jesus. He has given us authority to deliver the captives etc.

I coached kids' baseball for years and encountered some who were afraid to take a 'lead' off first base. Playing it too safe means you can't get to second base. My statement to them was that you can never reach the next base without first taking your foot off the one you are on. You can be out while standing safely on that first base if the batter behind you hits a ground ball.

Too many Christians are 'out' while playing it safe. We all do it sometimes, but we are admonished to forsake that 'posture.' Instead, we are to *"be imitators (followers) of God as beloved children." (Ephesians 5:1 NRSV)* We are to be *"doers of the word and not hearers only, deceiving our own selves." (James 1:22 KJV)*

It is time for church people today to put on the mantle the Holy Spirit gives and 'show and tell.' Paul said to the Corinthians, *"I come not with enticing words of man's wisdom, but in demonstration of the Spirit and of power; that your faith should not stand in the wisdom of men, but in the power of God." (1 Corinthians 2:4,5 KJV)*

I believe we can do the same, if we are willing.

Faith is risky business. But it is rewarding.

"And the life which I now live

in the flesh, I live

by the faith of the Son

of God, who loved me,

and gave himself

for me."

(Galatians 2:20b KJV)

Questions
for Personal Reflection:

Have you found yourself encouraged that God was going to establish something for you, then looked at your circumstances, saw the improbability of your achieving it, and decided that it must not be God?

Are you familiar with the authority we have been given in Jesus' name? Would you like to know more about the authority of the believer? (For more information, contact me.)

"But be doers of the word, and not mearly hearers who deceive themselves."

James 1:22 NRSV

16

Believe and Declare

Once upon a time in heaven, there lived with God an archangel named Lucifer. He was created with extreme beauty and musical gifts and was made a leader by the Monarch of heaven. Lucifer is described in Ezekiel 28:13-19.

Lucifer led the angels and archangels in worshiping God, but he became prideful and felt he didn't need to bow before God. He thought more highly of himself than he ought. Just like many humans. Therefore, God kicked him out of heaven and created hell for Lucifer's (Satan's) eternal abode. And for every being who chooses to follow his ways.

Ephesians tells us we all formerly conducted ourselves *"according to the (ways, attitudes) of this world."* Pride kept us from understanding that our attitudes and actions put us at odds with God and we needed to be reconciled to Him. Reconciled means to be at peace and in harmony with God. Until we are, our conduct is like that of *"the prince of the power of the air, the spirit that now works in the children of disobedience." (Ephesians 2:2 NKJV)* Satan is that prince. We all once followed his example, being prideful and disobedient and disrespectful of the things of

God.

But that's easy to change. *"For if you confess with your lips that Jesus is Lord, and believe in your heart that God raised Him from the dead, you will be saved. For one believes with the heart and so is justified, and one confesses with the mouth, and so is saved."(Romans 10:9,10 NRSV)*

If you've never settled that question about your present and eternal destiny, you can do so on your own right now. *"The scripture says, No one who believes in Him will be put to shame."(Romans 10:11 NRSV)* Speak aloud that you believe God raised Jesus from the dead, then kill pride's dominance by telling someone about your decision.

God opened the door through Jesus. Enter into His kingdom by stepping through that door right now. Don't put it off!

Welcome to the family of God. *"For our sake he made Him to be sin who knew no sin, so that in Him we might become the righteousness of God." (2 Corinthians 5:21 NRSV)* It's a great life!

Questions
for Personal Reflection:

✖ Have you accepted Jesus as your personal Savior and submitted to Him as Lord over your life?

About the Author

Grider Thrasher has been on a journey of faith for most of his life, but he readily admits to often being tossed to and fro by winds of doubt and uncertainty. *"A moment of speaking doubt,"* he says, *"can undo weeks of standing in faith."* (James 1:6-8 my paraphrase)

He shares some of his more successful experiences of that life's journey in this book as an encouragement to others who have struggled to hear God and obey His voice. He hastens to say that he shares not as one who has arrived, but as one who is still determined to fulfil God's plans and purposes for his own life.

Married to one wife, Sally since 1957, he has two married sons and five grandchildren.

Grider has a broad range of life's experiences, including pastoral and traveling ministry, ministry for television on both sides of the camera, television news, sportswriter, business owner, and sales. He also has written books on volunteer leadership development for The United States Jaycees and conducted leadership seminars throughout the United States.

He has traveled to most of the U.S. and to Canada and Costa Rica. and done short-term mission ventures to parts of northern Mexico. He has ministered among Muslims in Spain and Morocco, and taught Bible truths and the work of the Holy Spirit on several trips to Russia.

Grider is still available for ministry in local churches and on mission assignments.

The journey of faith continues...

Contact Me

at

Grider Thrasher

(870) 926- 3647

or E-mail

pop4gospel2u@suddenlink.net